# PIECES OF
# SHADOW

TEZONTLE

FONDO DE CULTURA ECONÓMICA
FUNDACIÓN PARA LAS LETRAS MEXICANAS

First Edition (FCE), 2007

Originally published in 1995 by Papeles Privados, S. C.

Sabines, Jaime
    Pieces of Shadow. Selected Poems / Jaime Sabines ; trad. de
W. S. Merwin. – México : FCE, Fundación para las Letras Mexicanas,
2007
    131 p. ; 21 x 14 cm — (Colec. Tezontle)
    Selección de Nuevo recuento de poemas
    ISBN 978-968-16-7897-5

    I. Poesía Mexicana 2. Literatura Mexicana – Siglo XX
I. Merwin, W. S., tr. II. Ser. III. t.

LC PQ72 97                                     Dewey M861 S712p

This book was published with the assistance of Fundación para las Letras
Mexicanas, A. C. / Esta obra se realizó gracias al apoyo de la Fundación
para las Letras Mexicanas, A. C.

Comments or suggestions: editorial@fondodeculturaeconomica.com
Visit our website and catalogue: www.fondodeculturaeconomica.com

**fce** Certified ISO 9001:2000

Worldwide Distribution

Printed on acid-free paper by
Impresora y Encuadernadora Progreso, S. A. de C. V. (IEPSA)

Printed in Mexico | Impreso en México

# PIECES OF SHADOW

## SELECTED POEMS

Jaime Sabines

•

Translated by
W. S. Merwin

# Contents

*Translator's Note*   15


*Horal* (1950)
    *Slow, bitter animal*   21
    *I don't know it for certain. . .*   23
    *One is the man*   24
    *Site of love. . .*   26
    Mezzanine   28
    The Lovers   30


*The Signal* (1951)
    On the Heart of Man   35
    On Hope   36
    On Night   37
    On Illusion   38
    On Death   39
    On Good-bye   40
    On Myth   41
    At this Time, Here   42
    *I've seen them at the movies*   44

Aunt Chofi   46
*Wanting to cry. . .*   49


*Adam and Eve* (1952)
   IV   53
   VII   54
   X   55


*Tarumba* (1956)
   *Tarumba*   59
   *People and things go into the house of day*   60
   *On horseback, Tarumba*   61
   *If anyone tells you. . .*   63
   *What the hell can I do. . .*   64
   *Broken like a plate*   65
   *After reading so many pages. . .*   66
   *Here comes a subterranean gallop*   68


*Weekly Diary and Poems in Prose* (1961)
   *I love you at ten in the morning. . .*   73
   *Reading Tagore. . .*   74
   *If I were going to die in a moment. . .*   75
   *I take pleasure in the way the rain beats. . .*   77
   *I am my body. . .*   78
   *At midnight. . .*   79
   *Before long you will offer these pages. . .*   80
   *They amble along the old avenue. . .*   81

*Collected Poems* (1961)
    *You have what I look for...* 85
    The Paralytic    86
    *With the nerves coming out of my body...* 87
    *Here we are...* 90
    *I'm out to find a man...* 92
    *I have eyes to see...* 93
    *From the blue and black bodies* 94
    *Surrounded by butterflies...* 95

*Yuria* (1967)
    *What a barbarous custom...* 99
    *We ought to confer sainthood...* 100
    *I left my corpse...* 102

*Badtime* (1972)
    *I'm worried about the television...* 107
    The Mountains    108
    The Official Daily    110

*Loose Poems* (1981)
    The Pedestrian    113
    Considering it Carefully    114
    The Moon    115
    Message to Rosario Castellanos    117
    Sisyphus    119
    The Sphinx    120
    Family    121

Horsepower  122
The Crazy Tomcat  123

*Other Collected Poems* (1950-1995)
    *Hallelujah to mother!. . .*  127
    *The one without teeth*  128
Job's Worry  130

*Bibliography*  131

# Translator's Note

It must have been Mark Strand who first showed me some poems by Jaime Sabines to see whether I might translate them for *New Poetry of Mexico*, the bilingual anthology that he was putting together, which was eventually published by Dutton in 1970. At about the same time Janet Brof showed me others, when she and Hortense Carpentier were assembling their anthology of Latin-American prose and poetry *Doors and Mirrors*, which Grossman published in 1972. It is hard to believe that my first acquaintance with those poems, and the work on them and on others that followed, and the association spiralling out of them, took place that long ago. There are probably a number of reasons for that apparent closeness, but one of them certainly is in the fact that many of the poems by Sabines that I was most drawn to at that time seem to me as strong and vivid now as they did then. They seem unchanged. Which permits the illusion that I must not have changed either.

Sabines had published his first book of poems, *Horal*, in 1950, when he was twenty five, and his first collected volume, *Recuento de poemas*, representing four earlier books and an imposing group of subsequent poems, in 1962. Many of his poems that I still return to with admiration and particular pleasure are from that first collection still. What impresses me about them, as it does about those poems of his that have most struck me in later years, is the jarring authenticity of passion in their tone, a great cracked bell note of craving and frustration, irony and anger, outrage and black humor all jangled at once, unabashed, unsweetened, unappeased, and all of it essential to the rest. I was caught first, as one must be almost inevitably by poems, I believe, by individual pieces, lines, phrases that rang with an authority that seemed to me indisputable. It was there for me in such poems as "On Myth"

> My mother told me that I cried in her womb.
> They said to her: he'll be lucky.

> Someone spoke to me every day of my life,
> into my ear, slowly, taking their time.
> Said to me: live, live, live!
> It was death.

and

> I'm out to find a man who looks like me
> to give him my name and my wife and my son,
> my books and my debts.
> I'm going looking for someone to give him my soul,
> my fate, my death.

> With what pleasure I'd do it,
> with what tenderness I'd leave myself in his hands!

But then there were erotic poems of a wry and wholly credible intimacy and tenderness, above all the one that begins

*You have what I look for, what I long for, what I love,*
*you have it.*
*The fist of my heart is beating, calling.*
*I thank the stories for you.*
*I thank your mother and your father*
*and death who has not seen you.*
*I thank the air for you.*
*You are elegant as wheat,*
*delicate as the outline of your body.*
*I have never loved a slender woman*
*but you have made my hands fall in love,*
*you moored my desire,*
*you caught my eyes like two fish.*
*And for this I am at your door, waiting.*

And the range of tone and panorama in the poems in prose, from elegiac compassion to matured scorn, which added to my sense of a complex sensibility, a full and rounded gift.

I got Sabines' later books when they appeared, and many poems from them became part of the response I felt to the work of his that I already knew. For several years I would often take a book of Sabines' poems with me when I travelled. And still he remains elusive, surprising, and like no one else. I am grateful to him for these years of words —hoarse, angry, bitter, affectionate, vibrant— that have the inexplicable power not only to survive themselves, but to give life in turn.

W. S. MERWIN

# Horal
(1950)

SLOW, BITTER ANIMAL
that I am, that I have been,
bitter since the tangle of dust and water and wind
that, in the first generation of man, asked something of God.

Bitter like those bitter minerals
that in the nights of exact solitude
—accursed and ruined solitude
without oneself—
climb the throat
and, crusts of silence,
suffocate, kill, revive.

Bitter like that bitter voice
before birth, before matter, that said
our word, that walked our path,
that died our death,
and that we discover in each moment.

Bitter from inside,
from what I am not,
—my skin as my tongue
from the first life
herald and prophecy.

Slow for centuries,
remote —there is nothing behind—,
far away, far off, unknown.

Slow, bitter animal
that I am, that I have been.

I DON'T KNOW IT FOR CERTAIN, BUT I IMAGINE
that a man and a woman
fall in love one day,
little by little they come to be alone,
something in each heart tells them that they are alone,
alone on the earth they enter each other,
they go on killing each other.

It all happens in silence. The way
light happens in the eye.
Love unites bodies.
They go on filling each other with silence.

One day they wake up, over their arms.
Then they think they know the whole thing.
They see themselves naked and they know the whole thing.

(I'm not sure about this. I imagine it.)

ONE IS THE MAN.
One knows nothing about those things
that the poets, the blind, whores
call "mystery" and are afraid of and cry about.
One was born naked, dirty,
straight into the wet,
and did not drink metaphors for milk
and lived nowhere except on earth
(The earth which is the earth and is heaven
as the rose is a rose but a stone).

One is scarcely a sure thing
that lets itself live, scarcely die,
and forgets each moment so
that each moment is new, and surprising.

One is something that lives,
something that looks but finds,
something like a man or like God or grass
that in the hard knowledge of this world
finds the miracle in the first place.

JAIME SABINES

Time is easy now, death is easy,
easy and rigorous and true
each intention of love that lives in us
and each solitude that performs us.
It's all here, here. And the heart learns
—happiness and sorrow— all presence;
the constant heart, balanced and good,
empties and fills.

One is the man who walks the earth
and finds the light and says: it is good.
Sees it and knows it and takes it
to the branch of a tree, to the river, to the city,
to dreams, and hope, and waiting.

One is that destiny that sometimes
penetrates the skin of God
and he fades into everything and dissolves.

One is the water of his own thirst,
the silence that hushes our tongue,
the bread, the salt, the amorous urge
of the air stirring in every cell.

One is a man —the word they used for him—
who sees it all open, and says nothing, and goes in.

SITE OF LOVE, PLACE WHERE I HAVE LIVED
at a distance, you, unknown,
beloved whom I kept silent, gaze that I have not seen,
lie that I was told and have never believed:

in this hour in which we two, without being both,
in grieving and hatred and death loved each other,
I am, or am I —if only I were!—
loving you, crying for myself, lost.

(This is the last time I will love you.
I tell you this and I mean it.)

Things I don't know, have never learned,
with you, now, here, I have learned them.

In you my heart grew.
In you my anguish was formed.
Beloved, place where I come to rest,
silence in which I suffer.

(When I look at your eyes
there's a child in my mind.)

JAIME SABINES

There are hours, hours, hours, in which you are as absent
as all I tell you.

Your heart at the surface of your skin, your hands,
your smile lost around a cry,

this heart of yours again, so poor, so plain,
and this step of yours looking for me where I have not gone:

all this that you do and don't do sometimes
is like a way of fighting with you.

Girl of the horrors, my fallen heart,
you see now, girl, my love, the things I say.

# Mezzanine

A wardrobe, a mirror, a chair,
not one star, my room, a window,
the night as always, and I, not hungry,
chewing gum, dreaming, hoping.
There are a lot of men outside, everywhere,
and beyond them the fog, the morning.
There are frozen trees, dry earth,
fish motionless, indistinguishable from the water,
nests asleep under warm doves.
Here, no woman. I wish there were one.
For days now my heart has wanted to swell
under a caress, a word.
The night is harsh. The shadow drags itself
across the walls, slow as the dead.
That woman and I were fastened together with water.
Her skin over my bones
and my eyes in her glance.
We have died many times
by daybreak.
I remember that I remember her name,
her lips, her skirt that I could see through.

Her breasts are sweet, and from one place
on her body to another it is a long way:
from nipple to nipple a hundred lips and an hour,
from pupil to pupil a heart, two tears.
I love her to the bottom of all the abysses,
to the last flight of the last wing,
when all the flesh is no longer flesh, nor the soul
    soul.
One has to love. I've come to know that. I love her.
How hard, and warm, and clear she is!

I wish she were here tonight.
From the street the sound of a violin floats up.
Yesterday I watched two little boys combing their hair
in front of naked dummies in a store window.
For three years I worried when I heard the whistle
    of the train,
now I know it is a machine.
No good-bye is better than the one of every day
to everything, to every moment, the blood
lit up on high.

Deserted blood, soft night,
tobacco of insomnia, mournful bed.

I'm going somewhere else.
And I'm taking my hand, that writes and talks so much.

# The Lovers

The lovers say nothing.
Love is the finest of the silences,
the one that trembles most and is hardest to bear.
The lovers are looking for something.
The lovers are the ones who abandon,
the ones who change, who forget.
Their hearts tell them that they will never find.
They don't find, they're looking.

The lovers wander around like crazy people
because they're alone, alone,
surrendering, giving themselves to each moment,
crying because they don't save love.
They worry about love. The lovers
live for the day, it's the best they can do, it's all they know.
They're going away all the time,
all the time, going somewhere else.
They hope,
not for anything in particular, they just hope.
They know that whatever it is they will not find it.
Love is the perpetual deferment,
always the next step, the other, the other.

JAIME SABINES

The lovers are the insatiable ones,
the ones who must always, fortunately, be alone.

The lovers are the serpent in the story.
They have snakes instead of arms.
The veins in their necks swell
like snakes too, suffocating them.
The lovers can't sleep
because if they do the worms eat them.

They open their eyes in the dark
and terror falls into them.

They find scorpions under the sheet
and their bed floats as though on a lake.

The lovers are crazy, only crazy
with no God and no devil.

The lovers come out of their caves
trembling, starving,
chasing phantoms.
They laugh at those who know all about it,
who love forever, truly,
at those who believe in love as an inexhaustible lamp.

The lovers play at picking up water,
tattooing smoke, at staying where they are.
They play the long sad game of love.
None of them will give up.
The lovers are ashamed to reach any agreement.

Empty, but empty from one rib to another,
death ferments them behind the eyes,
and on they go, they weep toward morning
in the trains, and the roosters wake into sorrow.

Sometimes a scent of newborn earth reaches them,
of women sleeping with a hand on their sex, contented,
of gentle streams, and kitchens.

The lovers start singing between their lips
a song that is not learned.
And they go on crying, crying
for beautiful life.

# The Signal
(1951)

# On the Heart of Man

By now I have seen many things on the earth
and only the heart of man was painful to see.
It dreams and never rests.
It has no house in the world.
It's alone.
It leans on God or falls upon death
but never rests.

The heart of man dreams
and walks alone on earth
the length of the days, without end.

It's a bad deal.

# On Hope

Occupy yourselves here with hope.
The joy of the day that's coming
buds in your eyes like a new light.
But that day that's coming isn't going to come: this is it.

JAIME SABINES

# On Night

In the amorous night I pine.
I ask it its secret, my secret.
I question my blood in detail.
It doesn't answer
and acts like my mother,
who shuts my eyes without hearing me.

# On Illusion

On the tablet of my heart you wrote:
desire.
And I walked for days and days
mad and scented and dejected.

# On Death

Bury it.
There are many silent men under the earth
who will take care of it.
Don't leave it there.
Bury it.

# On Good-bye

It's not said.
It gets to our eyes,
our hands, trembles, struggles.
You say that you wait —and you wait— from then on
and you know that good-bye is of no use and is sad.

# On Myth

My mother told me that I cried in her womb.
They said to her: he'll be lucky.

Someone spoke to me all the days of my life,
into my ear, slowly, taking their time.
Said to me: live, live, live!
It was death.

# At this Time, Here

I ought to dance to that *danzón* they're playing down
   in the cabaret,
leave my cooped up room
and go down dancing among the drunks.
A man's a fool to lie in bed
without a woman, bored, thinking,
just thinking.
I'm not "starved for love", but I don't want
to spend every night in a soak,
staring at my arms,
or with the light out, making drawings with a lit cigarette.
Reading, or remembering,
or admiring my literary status,
or waiting for something.
I ought to go down into the empty street
and with my hands in my pockets, slowly
go along with my feet, saying to them:
one, two, three, four...
This Mexican sky is dark,
full of cats,
with frightened stars
and wrung out air.

JAIME SABINES

(Last night it had rained, though,
and turned cool, amorous, thin.)
I ought to spend today crying
on a wet sidewalk at the foot of a tree,
or wait for a shameful streetcar
and shout at it, at the top of my voice.
If I had a dog I could pet it.
If I had a child I would show him my picture
or tell him a story
that didn't mean a thing but was long.
I don't want, now, no I don't want
to keep lying awake night after night.
When am I going to get to sleep, when?
What I want is for something to happen.
To die, for real,
or really be fed up,
or at least have the roof of my house
fall for a while.

Let the cage tell me about its affair with the canary.
Let the poor moon that the gypsies still sing to
and the tender moon of my cupboard
say something to me,
talk to me in metaphors the way they're supposed to.
This wine is bitter.
I have a beetle under my tongue.

How nice if my room
were left to itself all night,
turned into a fool, staring!

I'VE SEEN THEM AT THE MOVIES,
in front of the theaters,
in the streetcars and in the parks,
fingers and eyes tight.
In the dark halls girls offer
their breasts to hands
and open their mouths for the wet caress
and spread their thighs for unseen satyrs.
I've seen them make love to themselves in expectation,
    imagining
the pleasure their clothes are covering, the falseness
of the sweet talk they want to hear,
strangers to each other.
It's the flower that opens
through the longest day,
the heart that hopes,
trembling like a blind man in a prophecy.

That girl I saw today was fourteen,
beside her, her parents watched her laughter
as though she had stolen it.

Often I have watched them,
the lovers,
on the sidewalks, on the grass, under a tree,
meeting in the flesh,
sealing with their lips.
And I have seen the black sky
in which there are no birds,
and structures of steel
and poor houses, patios,
forgotten places.
And they're trembling constantly,
they put themselves in their hands,
and love smiles, moves them, instructs them
like an old disillusioned grandfather.

# Aunt Chofi

It was a sad dawn, the day you died, Aunt Chofi,
but that afternoon I went to the movies and made love.
I did not know that, a thousand leagues from here,
    you were dead
all seventy years of you, a virgin to the end,
stretched out on your cot, stupidly dead.
You were right to die, Aunt Chofi,
because you weren't doing anything, nobody paid
    any attention to you,
because after grandma died, to whom you'd devoted your life,
you had nothing to do, and it was plain from a long way off
that you wanted to die and were just hanging on.
You were right to die!
I don't want to sing your praises the way people do
    who are sorry,
because I loved you in your time, in a specific place,
and I know quite well what you were, how ordinary,
    how simple,
but I've started crying like a girl because you died.
You seem so forsaken to me,
so alone, with nobody to help you at the corner,
nobody to bring you some bread!

JAIME SABINES

I hate to think of you under the ground,
so cold there in Berriozábal,
alone, alone, horribly alone,
crying as though I'd die.
I know it's silly. You're dead.
It would make more sense to be quiet.
But what can I do
if your death hits me harder than I thought it would?

Oh humpbacked Aunt Chofi
I wish you would sing
or tell about your love life.
The peasants who buried you had nothing
but drinks and cigarettes,
and that's all I have.
Heaven must be finished with your death now,
and a just and benevolent God must have picked you out.
Never was all that you believed so real.
You had so little that you ended up giving your life
to everybody. Destitute, you begged so you could give.
And were not sour in the way of spinsters
for your virginity was like a teeming pregnancy.
Square in the middle of the two or three ideas that filled
    your life
you repeated yourself tirelessly
always the same.
Easy, like the flowers of the field
which the neighbors sprinkled on your coffin,
you were never so well off as in that forsakeness of death.
Sofia, virgin, old devoted woman,
they should have buried you in white
for your definitive wedding.

You who never knew a man's caress
and who let wrinkles come to your face before
     there were kisses,
you, chaste, clean, sealed,
should be carrying orange blossoms on your last day.
I demand that the angels take you
and lead you to the abode of the clean.
Virgin Sofia, transparent vase, calyx,
may death gather your head tenderly
and close your eyes with a mother's care
humming songs that have no end.
You will be forgotten by everyone
like the lilies of the field
and the solitary stars,
but in the mornings, in the breath of the ox,
in the trembling of the plants,
in the mildness of the streams,
in the nostalgia of the cities,
you will be like the untouchable mist, the breath
     of God waking.

Virgin Sofia, married in a country cemetery
with a small cross over your bit of earth,
you are all right where you are, under the birds
     of the mountain
and under the grass that makes you a curtain
     to watch the world through.

WANTING TO CRY, ALMOST IN TEARS,
I draw to my youth, over my arms,
the cloth of my blood in which
my heart rests with its hopes.

Here, weak, convalescent, alien,
deaf to my voice, marked
with a sign of dread,
I arrive at my youth like the leaves
that the wind keeps spinning around the tree.

Few words I learned
to speak of the rare
event of my ruin:
shadow and wound,
lust, thirst and crying.

I arrive at my youth and spill over
its edge like an angry liquid,
like the blood of a beautiful horse,
like the water in the thighs
of a woman with her thighs tight together.

My youth does not sustain me and I don't know
what I say and what I don't say.
In my tenderness I'm like
the eyelids in sleep
and when I walk I'm like the blind
learning the way through their footsteps.

Leave me here. I'm happy. I'm waiting for something.
All I need is a high
dream and a collapse that never stops.

Adam and Eve
(1952)

# IV

——Yesterday I was watching the animals and I got to thinking about you. Females are smoother, softer, and more mischievous. Before yielding themselves they give the males a hard time, or they run away, they defend themselves. Why? I have seen you too, like the doves, making yourself excited when I am quiet. Is it that your blood and mine heat up at different times?

Now when you are asleep is when you should answer me. Your breath is calm and your face has let go and your lips are apart. You could say it all without affliction and without laughing.

Are we really different? Weren't you made, after all, out of my rib, aren't you what hurts me?

When I'm in you, when I make myself little and you put your arms around me and wrap yourself around me and close up like a flower with an insect, I know something, we know something. The female is always bigger, in some way.

We save ourselves from death. Why? Every night we save ourselves. We stay together, arms around each other, and I begin to grow like the day.

I must be looking for something in you, something of mine that you are and that you are never going to give me.

Why did they separate us? I need you, to be able to walk, to be able to see, like a third eye, like another foot that only I know I have.

# VII

—What is the song of the birds, Adam?

—It's the birds themselves turning into air. Singing is spilling out into drops of air, threads of air, trembling.

—So the birds are ripe, and their throats fall like leaves, and their leaves are soft, penetrating, sometimes quick. Why? Why am I not ripe?

—When you are ripe you will let go of yourself and the part of you that is fruit will be happy and the part that is branch will keep trembling. Then you will know. The sun has not entered you as it has the day. You are dawning.

—I want to sing. I have an air that I am holding tight, a bird's air, my own air. I am going to sing.

—You are always singing and don't know it. You are like the water. The stones don't know it either, and their silent lime comes together and sings silently.

# X

We went to the sea. How frightened I was, and how happy! It is a huge, restless animal. It lashes out and it blows, it gets angry, it quiets down, it's always frightening. It's as though it were watching us from inside, from the depths, with many eyes, eyes like the ones we have in the heart that allow us to look a long way into the darkness.

At first it knocked us down a few times. Then Adam got angry and started to hit the waves with his fist. That made me laugh. I stayed on the beach watching. Adam couldn't do a thing. Before long he came out of the water, tired, wet, and didn't say anything, and went to sleep.

Then I started to listen to the sea. It was getting dark. It sounds like the night. A vast, infinite silence, a deep voice. It spreads out its dark sound and enters us from all sides. It's the sound of the weight of water, of water trying to get up like a wounded animal.

From now on we will live beside the sea. Here the sun and the sea are at the same height, the stars and the big fish are at the same depth.

We will learn the sea. It has its mountains and its plains, its birds, its minerals, its unanimous and difficult vegetation. We will learn its changes, its seasons, the way it is fixed in the world like a huge root, the root of the tree of water that wrings the earth, the enormous tree that reaches out into space forever.

The sea is good and terrible like my father. I want to call it father sea. Father sea, hold me up, create me again in your heart. Make me incorruptible, receiver of the world, purifier in spite of everything.

Tarumba
(1956)

TARUMBA.
I go with the ants
among the feet of the flies.
I go with the ground, through the wind,
in the shoes of men,
in the cloven hooves, the leaves, the papers;
I go where you go, Tarumba,
where you come from, I'm coming.
I know the spider.
I know what you know of yourself
and what your father knew.
I know what you've told me of me.
I'm afraid not to know,
to be here like my grandmother
looking at the wall, good and dead.
I want to go out and piss in the moonlight.
Tarumba, it looks like rain.

PEOPLE AND THINGS GO INTO THE HOUSE OF DAY,
weeds that smell bad,
horses with wide eyes,
airs with music,
manikins like girls;
you go in, Tarumba, and I do.
The dance goes in. The sun goes in.
An insurance agent
and a poet.
A policeman.
We're all going to sell ourselves, Tarumba.

ON HORSEBACK, TARUMBA,
you need a horse
to get around this country,
to know your woman,
to want the one you want,
to open up the pit of your death,
to raise up your resurrection.
On horseback with your eyes,
the psalm of your eyes,
the sleep in your tired legs.
On horseback in the malarial region,
the sick time,
hot female,
dripping laughter.
Where the news of virgins arrive,
newspapers with saints,
and telegrams with hearts athletic as a flag.
On horseback, Tarumba, over the river,
over the slab of water, the vigil,
the fragile leaf of the dream
(when your hands wake up holding a bottom),
and the window of death in which you see
your little heart.

On horseback, Tarumba,
ride on to the sinkhole of the sun.

IF ANYONE TELLS YOU YOU CAN'T BE SURE
tell him to come
and put his hands on his gut and swear
and bear witness to the truth of everything.
To look at the light in the oil on the street,
the motionless automobiles,
the people passing and passing,
the four doors opening toward the east,
the riderless bicycles,
the bricks, the loving mortar,
the shelves falling at your back,
your father's gray hair,
the son your wife doesn't have,
and the money that enters with a mouthful of shit.
Tell him to swear in the name of God, unconquered
in the tournament of democracies,
that he's seen and heard.
Because he still has to listen to the crime of the cats
and a monstrous watch they're winding is held to your ear.

WHAT THE HELL CAN I DO WITH MY KNEE,
with my leg that's so long and scrawny,
with my arms, my tongue,
with my weak eyes?
What can I do in this whirlwind
of well-meaning imbeciles?
What can I do with the smart rotten ones
and with the sweet girls who don't love men but poetry?
What can I do with the poets wearing the uniforms
of the academy or of communism?
What, among hucksters or politicians
or the shepherds of souls?
What the hell can I do, Tarumba,
if I'm neither a saint nor a hero nor a bandit,
nor an adorer of art
nor a druggist
nor a rebel?
What can I do if I can do it all
and all I want is to look and look?

BROKEN LIKE A PLATE,
broken with desires, nostalgias, dreams,
I'm the guy who loves what's-her-name on the thirteenth of
    each month
and the guy who cries for the other one and the other one
    when he remembers them.
What a hunger for grown-up women
and for tender women!
My right arm wants a waist
and my left arm a head.
My mouth wants to bite and kiss and dry tears.
I go from pleasure to tenderness
in the house of the madman,
and I light candles
and burn my fingers like incense
and sing from my breast a raucous dark song.
I'm lost and broken
and I have nothing and nobody
and can't talk and it would do no good.
All I can do is to stir
while ash and stones
and shadows fall on me.

AFTER READING SO MANY PAGES THAT TIME WRITES WITH MY
   hand
I'm sad, Tarumba, not to have said more,
I'm sad to be so small
and I'm sad and angry not to be alone.
I'm sick of being all day long in the hands of people,
I hate the way they fling themselves onto me and flatten me
and don't even let me know what happened to my arms,
or see whether my legs are all there.
"Forsake father and mother"
and your wife and your son and your brother
and get into your sack of bones
and start rolling, if you're going to be a poet.
Don't be the slave of your navel or your blood,
nor of good or evil
nor of habitual love.
You have to act everything.
You have to break your head every day
on a stone, for the water to flow.
And afterward you'll be dragged to the side
like an empty bag
(leather glove once worn by the hand of poetry)
but you'll be dragged away also for nothing.

JAIME SABINES

66

Tarumba, I'm sick of serving poetry and the devil.
And sometimes I'm like my son who wets his bed
and can't move, and cries.

HERE COMES A SUBTERRANEAN GALLOP,
here comes a breaking sea,
here comes a sudden wind from Mars.
(Somebody has to explain to me
why so many things don't happen.)
Here comes a beat of blood
out of my mud feet,
here come gray hairs looking for my age,
boards floating for my coffin.
(The King of Kings eats an ear of corn as he waits,
trying on a pair of banana-leaf sandals.)
Comes my grandma Chus,
just turned unthirteen,
thirteen years in death,
thirteen years backward, downward.
Tony visits me, Chente, my aunt Chofi,
and other buried friends.
I think of Tito, pulling at the sleeve of his death,
and death paying no attention.
Here comes sad Chayito
with her mint leaf
and a little horse for my son.

JAIME SABINES

And here comes the heaviest rain of all time
and the fear of lightning
and I have to climb onto an ark turned into an ox
for the happy life that is waiting for us.

Weekly Diary and Poems in Prose
(1961)

I LOVE YOU AT TEN IN THE MORNING, at eleven, at twelve noon. I love you with my whole soul and my whole body, sometimes, on rainy afternoons. But at two in the afternoon, or at three, when I start to think about the two of us, and you are thinking about dinner or the day's work, or the amusements you don't have, I start to hate you with a dull hatred, with half of the hatred that I reserve for myself.

Then I go back to loving you, when we go to bed and I feel that you are made for me, that in some way your knee and your belly are telling me that, that my hands are assuring me of that, and that there is nowhere I can come to or go to that is better than your body. The whole of you comes to meet me and for a moment we both disappear, we put ourselves into the mouth of God, until I tell you that I am hungry or sleepy.

Every day I love you and hate you irreparably. And there are days, besides, there are hours, in which I don't know you, in which you are as strange to me as somebody else's wife. Men worry me, I worry about myself, my troubles bewilder me. Probably there is a long time when I don't think about you at all. So you see. Who could love you less than I do, my love?

READING TAGORE, this is what I thought: the lamp, the path, the pitcher in the well, my bare feet, are a lost world. Here are the light bulbs, the cars, the water faucet, the jet planes. Nobody tells stories. The television and the movies have replaced grandparents, and all of technology approaches the miraculous in order to announce soap and toothpaste.

I don't know how to get there, but we have to reach that tenderness of Tagore's and of all of oriental poetry, and have the girl with the pitcher of water on her shoulder instead of the efficient and impoverished typist. After all, we have the same clouds and the same stars, and if we think of it for a moment, the same sea.

The girl in the office wants love too. And in the midst of the chaos of papers that defile her every day there are leaves of white dreams that she saves carefully, clippings of tenderness toward which she ventures when she is alone.

Some day I want to sing of this immense poverty of our life, this nostalgia for things that are simple, this luxurious voyage upon which we have embarked toward tomorrow without having loved yesterday enough.

JAIME SABINES

IF I WERE GOING TO DIE IN A MOMENT, I would write these words of wisdom: tree of bread and honey, rhubarb, cocacola, zonite, swastika. And then I would start to cry.

You can start to cry even at the word "toilet" if you want to cry.

And this is how it is with me now. I'm ready to give up even my fingernails, to take out my eyes and squeeze them like lemons over the cup of coffee. ("Let's have a cup of coffee with eye peel, my heart.")

Before the ice of silence descends on my tongue, before my throat splits and my heart keels over like a leather sack, I want to tell you, my life, how grateful I am for this stupendous liver that let me eat all your roses on the day when I got into your hidden garden without anyone seeing me.

I remember it. I filled my heart with diamonds —they are fallen stars that have aged in the dust of the earth— and it kept jingling like a tambourine when I laughed. The only thing that really annoys me is that I could have been born sooner and you didn't do it.

Don't put love into my hands like a dead bird.

I TAKE PLEASURE IN THE WAY THE RAIN BEATS ITS WINGS on the back of the floating city.

The dust comes down. The air is left clean, crossed by leaves of odor, by birds of coolness, by dreams. The sky receives the city that is being born.

Streetcars, buses, trucks, people on bicycles and on foot, carts of all colors, street-vendors, bakers, pots of *tamales*, grilles of baked bananas, balls flying between one child and another: the streets swell, the sounds of voices multiply in the last light of the day hung up to dry.

They come out like ants after the rain, to pick up the crumb of the sky, the little straw of eternity to take away to their dark houses, with cuttlefish hanging from the roofs, with weaving spiders under the beds, and with one familiar ghost, at least, in back of some door.

Thanks be to you, Mother of the Black Clouds, who have so whitened the face of the afternoon and have helped us to go on loving life.

I AM MY BODY. And my body is sad and tired. I'm ready to sleep for a week, a month. Not to be disturbed.

I hope that when I open my eyes my children will have grown and everything will be smiling.

I want to stop walking around barefoot in the cold. Cover me up with everything that's warm, the sheets, the blankets, a few papers and keepsakes, and close the door to keep my solitude in.

I want to sleep for a month, a year, go to sleep. And if I talk in my sleep don't pay any attention, if I say a name, if I complain. I want to be considered buried, so that there's nothing for you to do until resurrection day.

Now I want to sleep for a year, just sleep.

AT MIDNIGHT, at the last moment of August, I think sadly about the leaves that keep falling from the calendars. I feel that I am the tree of the calendars.

Every day, my child, that goes away forever, leaves me asking: if someone who loses a parent is an orphan, if someone who has lost a wife is a widower, what is the word for someone who loses a child? What is the word for someone who loses time? And if I myself am time, what is the word for me if I lose myself?

Day and night, not Monday or Tuesday, nor August or September, day and night are the only measure of our duration. To exist is to last, to open your eyes and close them.

Every night at this time, forever, I am the one who has lost the day. (Even though I may feel, in the heart of this time, the dawn climbing, like the fruit in the branches of the peach tree.)

BEFORE LONG YOU WILL OFFER THESE PAGES to people you don't know as though you were holding out a handful of grass that you had cut.

Proud and depressed of your achievement you will come back and fling yourself into your favorite corner.

You call yourself a poet because you don't have enough modesty to remain silent.

Good luck to you, thief, with what you're stealing from your suffering and your loves! Let's see what sort of image of yourself you make out of the pieces of your shadow you pick up.

THEY AMBLE ALONG THE OLD AVENUE, the Sunday flower tucked into their hair. Clean clothes, fresh out of the bath, combed and ironed, they walk among the children and the balloons and chatter and make friends and even listen to the music from the kiosk of the Alameda de Santa María that reassembles those who have survived the week.

The help, the servants, the girls who do the housework these days, give themselves over to it. The slide toward prostitution or go back to the bosom of some miserable family, but in the meantime they take the day off on Sunday, with its chance of a romance, its opportunity to dream. All they need is two or three hours wandering along vacantly to forget how tired they are and to face with a smile the looming dirty dishes, the laundry on the line and the calls for them that never stop.

Side by side with the old people who walk looking for their memories, and the ladies thinking about their next pregnancy, they relish their provisional freedom and possess the world, proud of their shoes and their pretty clothes and their hairdo that never looked so stunning.

(Lord, give us faith in Sunday. Let us believe in hair oil of one kind or another, and have the clean souls we need to look happily upon the days to come!)

Collected Poems
(1961)

YOU HAVE WHAT I LOOK FOR, WHAT I LONG FOR, WHAT I LOVE,
you have it.
The fist of my heart is beating, calling.
I thank the stories for you.
I thank your mother and your father
and death who has not seen you.
I thank the air for you.
You are elegant as wheat,
delicate as the outline of your body.
I have never loved a slender woman
but you have made my hands fall in love,
you moored my desire,
you caught my eyes like two fish.
And for this I am at your door, waiting.

# The Paralytic

He came to look and he remained still.
He doesn't move and he can't get up.
He has a black angel on his shoulder.
Day after day he lies prostrate
with his parched smile and his silence.
Even if he wanted to, even if he were crying
to run, he couldn't. His body
is his enemy, keeps him stuck.
What a stifled sob, what a moan!
He's taken root, planted like a tree,
with the trunk in the wind and shaking,
eyes coming out of his skin,
he has other bodies
nearby in the air, and he stays quiet.
A dark lead in his legs,
slowly he's growing a lead mushroom.
Because he's tied, moored,
his heart is freer than ever.

JAIME SABINES

WITH THE NERVES COMING OUT OF MY BODY, UNRAVELLING,
like the straws of an old broom,
and dragging across the floor, still hauling
the burden of my soul,
worn out, completely, more tired than my own legs,
sick of using my heart day after day,
here I am on this bed and at this time
waiting for the landslide,
the collapse that at any moment is going to bury me.
(You have to close your eyes as though you were going to sleep
and not move a single leaf of your body.
It can happen from one moment to the next:
becoming quiet.
Shawls of air revolve slowly,
dense shadows scrape the walls,
the sky sucks you up through the roof.)

Tomorrow you will wake up once more
to go on among the others.
And you will love the sun and the cold,
the cars, the trains,
the fashionable houses and the barns,
the walls to which the lovers paste themselves

&#128;

like decals as night comes on,
the lonely parks in which the losers wander
head down, and the dreams feel themselves come to rest,
and a boyfriend gropes for her under the skirt
while the siren of the ambulance announces
starting time at the death factory.
You will love the miraculous city and its dream of the country,
the river of the avenues lit by so many people wanting
    the same thing,
the open doorways of the bars, the surprises of the bookstores,
the tub full of flowers, the barefoot children
who do not want to be heroes of poverty,
and the marquees, the billboards,
the hurry of those with nowhere to go to.
You will love the asphalt and the garret
and the drainage pumps and the cranes
and the palaces and the first class hotels
and the lawns of the houses with guard dogs
and two or three people who are going to die too.
You will love the smells of frying
that attract the hungry at night like a light,
and your head will go off following the perfume
some woman leaves in the air like a suspended boa.
And you will love the rides of the amusement parks
where the poor come for the vertigo and the laughing,
and the zoo where everyone feels important,
and the hospital, where suffering makes more brothers
than poverty ever can.
And the foundling homes, and the day care centers where
    the children are playing
and all the places where tenderness appears like a bud
and everything leads you to give thanks.

JAIME SABINES

Run your hand over the skin of the furniture,
wipe off the mirrors where you've let the dust gather.
There are seeds trying to open everywhere.
(Life will blossom in you suddenly like scarlet fever.)

HERE WE ARE, TOGETHER AGAIN
in this house as in Noah's Ark.
Blanca, Irene, María and other girls,
Jorge, Eliseo, Óscar and Rafael...
Let's hurry up and get acquainted
and fuck and forget ourselves.
The ox, the tiger, the dove, the lizard and the donkey, we'll all
drink together, and clamber and trample on each other
at this hour that is about to sink in the flood of night.
Alcohol lightnings slice through the dark of the pupils
and thunder and music strike among the naked voices.
The house revolves and sails toward the high hours.
Who's holding your hand, Magdalena, sunk among
    the pillows?
What a beautiful job you have, taking your clothes off
and lighting up the room!
Make love with everything you know, my dove:
your skilled hands, your mouth, your eyes,
your expert heart.
Salome, here is the head of the day
so you can dance in front of all the eyes in flames.
Lesbia, be sure not to take from us one petal of your hands!

The house is going up in a whirlwind and the time is rising like a sourdough. Here we all are, fermented, the soul budding through the body everywhere!

I'M OUT TO FIND A MAN WHO LOOKS LIKE ME
to give him my name and my wife and my son,
my books and my debts.
I'm going looking for someone to give him my soul,
my fate, my death.

With what pleasure I'd do it,
with what tenderness I'd leave myself in his hands!

I HAVE EYES TO SEE IN THIS NIGHT
something of what I am, my hearing is hearing.
I am in this room, so are my dreams.

Back of each shadow there's something of mine.
There's one sitting on each chair, dark,
and at my feet, in bed, they're seeing me.
I believe they're like me, they bear my name
and they emerge from things, like mirrors.

It's already a long time
since we last assembled.
Now I give them lodging
humbly,
I give them my body.

I come together again at night, I open my eyes,
I wet them with this darkness full of dream.
Only my heart on top of the sheet
still beating.

FROM THE BLUE AND BLACK BODIES
that walk at times through my soul
come voices and signs that someone interprets.
It's dark as the sun
this desire. Mysterious and grave
as an ant dragging away the wing of a butterfly
or as the yes we say when things ask us
—do you want to live?

SURROUNDED BY BUTTERFLIES BLACK AS SOULS
and by the sharp daggers the dead use,
condescending to be a good man and a good soldier,
pater et filius admirabilis,
I canonize myself in the glorious dawn of the world.

I am the knower of mysteries,
the smiling sufferer,
the keeper of the keys of the stars.
I officiate at the zoo
before urban lions and monkeys with advanced
    degrees in psychology.
I am the King of the Civilized Forest,
container of the moon,
glass of happiness.

(North winds come with damp magnets
dragging and growing.
Birds lost like dreams.)

I am abandoned, Job's eczema,
my patience.

Yuria
(1967)

WHAT A BARBAROUS CUSTOM, this burying of the dead! Killing them, annihilating them, obliterating them from the face of the earth. It's betraying them, depriving them of the chance to revive.

I'm always hoping that the dead will rise up, that they'll break out of the coffin and say happily: What are you crying about?

So I'm nervous at funerals. They check the sections of the lid, they lower it all, they put flagstones on top of it, and then dirt, more, more, more, shovel after shovelful, clods, dust, stones, stamping on it, packing it down, flattening it, there you'll stay, you won't get out of here.

They make me laugh, after that, the crowns, the flowers, the crying, the unrestrained kisses. It's a joke. Why did they bury him? Why not leave him out to dry until his bones talked to us about his death? Or why not burn him, or give him to the animals, or throw him into the river?

There ought to be a rest home for the dead, airy and clean, with music and running water. There would be at least two or three, every day, who would rise up and live.

WE OUGHT TO CONFER SAINTHOOD UPON THE WHORES. Saturday's saints would be Betty, Lola, and Margot: perpetual virgins, reconstructed, provisory martyrs, full of grace, springs of generosity.

You give pleasure, oh whore, redeemer of the world, and you ask nothing in exchange but a few miserable coins. You don't demand to be loved, respected, taken care of, you don't imitate wives with their snivelling and their reproaches and jealousies. Nobody has to say good-bye to you or make up with you again. You don't suck blood or time. You are clean of guilt. You take sinners to your breast, listen to words and dreams, laugh and kiss. You are patient, expert, afflicted, wise, without rancor.

You don't cheat anybody, you are honest, genuine, complete. You state your price beforehand, you show yourself. You don't discriminate against the old, or against criminals or idiots or persons of another color. You put up with offenses of arrogance, the tricks of the sick. You relieve the impotent, arouse the timid, please those who have had enough, find a formula for the disillusioned. You are the drunkard's confidante, the refugee of the persecuted, the bed of the restless.

JAIME SABINES

You have trained your mouth and your hands, your muscles and your skin, your guts and your soul. You know how to dress and undress, go to bed, move. You are precise in your rhythm, exact in your moans, responsive in the ways of love.

You are freedom and balance. You do not force or detain anybody. You do not give in to memory or hope. You are pure presence, flow, perpetuity.

Whether the place where you practice the truth and beauty of life is an elegant brothel, a discreet house, or a bed in a hovel, you are a lamp and a glass of water and a loaf of bread.

Oh whore, my friend, my love, my beloved, eddy in this day of forever, I recognize you. Beside the hypocrites and perverts I pronounce you a saint. I give you my money. I crown you with leaves of grass and I get ready to learn from you all the time.

I LEFT MY CORPSE AT THE EDGE OF THE ROAD and I came on, crying for myself. The city is enormous, like an enormous orphanage. Cold and sheltering, dark and lit-up like jail.

I came looking for love. I thought that love was the only refuge from the night bombardments. And I found that love couldn't save itself. Love lasts only a moment. It is rotted by time, it can't survive absence, the hours make it rancid, it's the slave of the glands, it's naked to the weather.

My little garden was full of grubs. I couldn't find anything that I'd left there. Not a petal, not a thread of air.

Now what am I going to do? I want to cry, I'm crying. I want to get my things together again, a book, a box of matches, cigars, a pair of pants, maybe a shirt. I want to go away. I don't know where or what for, but I want to go away. I'm afraid. I'm unhappy.

What will become of my children? Oh I hope they grow up indifferent or ignorant. You have to get out of your mind. Rock and roll's good for that, and the twist, the mozambique.

JAIME SABINES

Do we have to stay drunk on something, as Baudelaire said? But this being lucidly drunk on time and people —isn't it too much?

I love you! I love you cockroach, Maria, Rosa, leprosy, Isabel, cancer, hepatitis, Gertrude, apple, butterfly, calf, walnut tree, river, meadow, cloud, mist, sun, black beetle, cardboard box, I love you, painted flower, plume, my love! I love you. I can't live without anybody. I'm going.

Badtime
(1972)

I'M WORRIED ABOUT THE TELEVISION. Its images, ultimately, are distorted. The faces are stretched until they're weird, or they shrink, or they shimmer out of focus and then turn into a monstrous game of invented faces, beams, lights and shadows, as in a nightmare. The words are perfectly distinct and the music and the sound effects, but they don't correspond to any reality. They're delayed, or they're too early, superimposed on the features that appear to be there.

I'm told that a repair man could fix it in two or three days, but I'm against that. I don't want violence. They'd put their hands inside there, take it apart, stick sinister things into it, risky transplants that might not take. It would never be itself again.

I really hope it gets over this. Because now it has a terrible temperature, a headache, awful nausea, which give it the dreams that we're watching.

# The Mountains

On the ranch of Orencio López, which is named El Carmen,
municipality of Ixhuatán, Chiapas, I knew the mountains.
The mountains exist. They are a mass of trees and water,
of a light that you can touch with your fingers,
and of something else that does not yet exist.

Pierced by the most solemn of airs,
nothing surpasses them at being earth,
centuries of hypnotized love, absorbed
in the creation and death of their leaves.

On the point of falling onto men,
miracle of balance, they remain
in their own place, they fall upward,
inside themselves, embrace themselves, the sky
    holds them up,
the day arrives at them, the night, the sounds,
clouds pass, and rivers, and storms,
they keep shadows that grow in hiding
among lyrical bamboos, they suckle
incredible lemons, they shepherd bushes and grasses,
they sleep standing on their own dream
of wood, of milk, of moistures.

JAIME SABINES

Here God stopped, stops,
holds off from himself, is content.

# The Official Daily
## (March, '70)

By presidential decree: the people doesn't exist.
The people is useful for speeches at banquets:
"I toast the people of Mexico."
"I toast the people of the United States."

And the people has other literary uses:
for writing the history of democracy,
publishing a review of the revolution,
making a chronicle of the great ideals.

The people is a pluperfect entity,
generously abstract and infinite.
And it's of use to help young idiots
add to the pantheons
or swell the jails
or learn how to get rich.

The Minister himself put it best:
"I wipe my ass with the people."
This is the best the people can hope to be:
a roll of toilet paper
of which they can write the history of our time
    with their nails.

JAIME SABINES

Loose Poems
(1981)

# The Pedestrian

It's said, it's rumored, it's asserted in the salons and at celebrations by somebody, or a number of people in the know, that Jaime Sabines is a great poet. Or at least a good poet. Or a decent poet, respectable. Or simply, but really, a poet.

The word reaches Jaime and it makes him happy. How wonderful! I'm a poet. I'm an important poet. I'm a great poet.

Convinced of it, he goes out into the street, or comes home. Convinced of it. But nobody in the street realizes that he's a poet, and even fewer at home. Why don't poets have a star on the forehead, or shine in some visible way, or have a ray coming out of their ears?

My God, Jaime said. I have to be Papa, or a husband, or work in a factory like anybody else, or walk, like anybody else. A pedestrian.

That's it, Jaime said. I'm not a poet, I'm a pedestrian.

And at that he lies on the bed with the sweet happiness of contentment.

# Considering it Carefully

They tell me I ought to exercise to lose weight,
that around 50 it's very dangerous to smoke and be fat,
it's important to keep your figure,
and fight against time and age.

Well-meaning experts and friends who are doctors
recommend diets and systems
for prolonging life for a few more years.

I thank them with all my heart but I have to laugh
at such vain dodges and petty concern.
(Death also laughs at all such things.)

The one bit of advice that I consider seriously
is to find a young woman to have in bed
because at this stage
youth can reach us only by contagion.

JAIME SABINES

# The Moon

You can take the moon by the spoonful
or in capsules every two hours.
It's useful as a hypnotic and sedative
and besides it relieves
those who have had too much philosophy.
A piece of moon in your purse
works better than a rabbit's foot.
Helps you find a lover
or get rich without anyone knowing,
and it staves off doctors and clinics.
You can give it to children like candy
when they've not gone to sleep,
and a few drops of moon in the eyes of the old
help them to die in peace.

Put a new leaf of moon
under your pillow
and you'll see what you want to.
Always carry a little bottle of air of the moon
to keep you from drowning.
Give the key to the moon
to prisoners and the disappointed.

For those who are sentenced to death
and for those who are sentenced to life
there is no better tonic than the moon
in precise and regular doses.

JAIME SABINES

# Message to Rosario Castellanos

*(Mexican poet who died in Israel in a household accident.*
*Translated Paul Claudel and St. J Perse into Spanish.)*

Only a fool could devote a whole life to solitude and love.
Only a fool could die by touching a lamp,
if a lighted lamp,
a lamp wasted in the daytime is what you were.
Double fool for being helpless, defenceless,
for going on offering your basket of fruit to the trees,
your water to the spring,
your heat to the desert,
your wings to the birds.
Double fool, double Chayito, mother twice over,
to your son and to yourself.
Orphan and alone, as in the novels,
coming on like a tiger, little mouse,
hiding behind your smile,
wearing transparent armor,
quilts of velvet and of words,
over your shivering nakedness.

How I love you, Chayo, how I hate to think
of them dragging your body, as I'm told they did.

Where did they leave your soul? Can't they
scrape it off the lamp,
get it up off the floor with a broom?
Don't they have brooms at the Embassy?
How I hate to think, I tell you, of them taking you,
laying you out, fixing you up, handling you,
dishonoring you with the funeral honors.
(Don't give me any of that
Distinguished Persons fucking stuff!)
I hate to think of it, Chayito! And is this all?
Sure it's all. All there is.
At least they said some good things in the paper
and I'm sure there were some who cried.
They're going to devote supplements to you,
poems better than this one, essays, commentaries.
How famous you are, all of a sudden!
Next time we talk
I'll tell you the rest.

I'm not angry now.
It's very hot in Sinaloa.
I'm going down to have a drink at the pool.

# Sisyphus

He flew from his peaceful life toward the light that had just been lit and his tiny body fell onto this sheet of paper I'm writing on.

I took away the coffee cup, thinking that what touched my lips might trouble it, and that a rain of invisible meteorites might start falling out of the center, through the star spaces, onto the table.

After a moment the body stirred, turned around slowly, moved its wings which grew lighter and lighter, and started to fly back. What a relief! What joy! Sisyphus of the light: I watched it rise in tight circles, swift and decisive, toward the glory of a new meeting with death.

# The Sphinx

The poor tree spent the whole night in the courtyard feeling cold, and now as day breaks it is raining, the dishwatery day of watery Mexico, enclosed like an egg, water all around, buses and people on the way to work, the gullets of the merciless schools swallowing children still in their sleep, stiff in the rainy hour of the day that doesn't move.

Only the cat understands. In its small, enormous world of the living room it gathers up its children with its eyes, lodges them in its paws, and turns into a sphinx, warm, timeless, perfect.

# Family

Since they were spending the whole morning house-cleaning, my daughters put out the dog, the cat, and their three children.

How come? Aren't they part of the human family?

No use my protesting. No use their meowing and barking and trying to sneak back in.

I'll go out to the patio and move in with them for a while.

# Horsepower

I just got my first luxury car. All my life I'd never had anything but little cars, nothing special, ordinary, what you could call tools of the trade.

Yesterday I was happy all day, like the time when I was eleven and got a bicycle.

What symbiosis takes place between the object and oneself? Why does the possession of the superfluous elevate the soul like a conquest?

It's as though the 240 horsepower increased one's own strength, one's capacity for action, one's power.

My wife and my children are happy too. We went around from one side to the other, admiring its impeccable upholstery, the gearshift on the floor, the side mirror that you could adjust from inside, and all the nice details that distinguished it.

My God, I said to myself, is this what they call infatuation, or is it the beginning of my decadence?

Well, I say to myself, to make me feel better: it'll take you two years to pay for it.

# The Crazy Tomcat

I libelled him. I called him the crazy tomcat. I said he needed a psychiatrist. I made dumb jokes about him.

When it starts to get dark, while the female cat picks out an easy chair in the living room, the cross-eyed tom starts his nightly round. He takes twelve or fourteen turns around my room, sticking close to the walls, under the bed, back of the chest of drawers, an unvarying, insistent itinerary. Then he goes out into the patio and spends the night, but I mean all night, going around and around it, meowing persistently, piteously, in a precise rhythm, as though he were looking for something or somebody, never giving up. His pace is quick, his posture alert, expectant.

At seven in the morning, more or less, he comes in to sleep. Every day the same.

I wondered whether he felt cooped up, or was anxious, or what. Now I've come to realize that it's just his job. He patrols the house against ghosts, bad vibrations, and extraterrestrials.

From now on I'll call him the night patrol, the dawn watch.

Other Collected Poems
(1950-1995)

HALLELUJAH TO MOTHER! HALLELUJAH TO TIME!
You have to feel the cold to know the wind is blowing.
A good drink and a good fire.
A good love between the legs.
Hallelujah to her! Hallelulight,
let time have an end!

Let the wind blow as it blows as it blows.
The cold keeps me in its mind.

Hands tied,
my body by the scruff,
the scruff a stick, the breath a windowpane.
What terrible cold,
what unimportance,
what desperation,
how fast,
how slow!

A coffee, please,
a brandy,
a puff on an ember,
a blanket, some linen...

**THE ONE WITHOUT TEETH**
can't dance.
The one without eyes
can't say "bon jour, Madame".
"Nice day.
Be so kind as to die."
The one with no pants
can't walk in the crowd.
The one without anybody
can't cry.
The one without anybody
can't cry. Can't cry. Can't cry.
(To be repeated three times.)

The one with no pillow
has to sleep on a whore's ass.
The one with no roof
will have to learn the alphabet of the stars.
The one with no wall
will have to stand up to the wind.
The one with no flesh
better go to the butcher.

JAIME SABINES

The one with no God:
to the church of the holy silence.

# Job's Worry

All of a sudden I feel persecuted by good luck. Everything is turning out right. I'm enjoying good health, and love, and money. What did I do? What can I do to deserve it?

My God, is this one more of your tests?

# Bibliography

*Horal*, Departamento de Prensa y Turismo, Tuxtla Gutiérrez, Chiapas, 1950.

*La señal*, Talleres de la Impresora Económica, México, 1951.

*Tarumba*, Colección Metáfora, México, 1956.

*Diario semanario y poemas en prosa*, Universidad Veracruzana, Xalapa, 1961 (Serie Ficción 27).

*En mis labios te sé*, Cuadernos del Cocodrilo 9, México, 1961.

*Recuento de poemas*, UNAM, México, 1962 (Col. Poemas y Ensayos).

*Yuria*, Mortiz, México, 1967 (Col. Las Dos Orillas).

*Maltiempo*, Mortiz, México, 1972 (Col. Las Dos Orillas).

*Algo sobre la muerte del Mayor Sabines*, Mortiz, México, 1973.

*Nuevo recuento de poemas*, Mortiz, México, 1977 (Col. Biblioteca Paralela).

*Poemas sueltos*, Papeles Privados, México, 1981.

*Otro recuento de poemas 1950-1991*, Mortiz, México, 1995.